Hector and Miranda are friends and classmates. They are both in the twelfth grade.

It is Saturday afternoon. Hector and Miranda are standing outside The Alamo Grill. The Alamo Grill is a restaurant. They are there for lunch. They are waiting for their friends Rafael and Eva. It's 12:20. Rafael and Eva are late.

Rafael and Eva finally arrive. They all sit down at a table outside. The friends talk before they order their food. Hector tells Miranda she should eat breakfast.

They keep talking. Rafael sleeps late on Saturdays. He usually gets up at eleven o'clock. At lunchtime on Saturday, he often eats breakfast.

The friends are still talking. Miranda is still hungry. She wants the potato soup and a very big sandwich. Hector wants a big salad and lots of bread.

They have delicious hamburgers here. You should order one.

A hamburger? No, thanks. I'm a vegetarian. I don't eat meat.

You're a vegetarian? You always eat vegetables? You never eat steak, chicken, or bacon?

That's right.

They talk some more. Rafael and Hector talk about the foods they eat. Hector doesn't eat meat because he is a vegetarian. He eats vegetables, beans, and rice. He sometimes eats eggs, milk, and cheese, but he never eats meat or fish.

Miranda wants to order. Hector calls the waiter.

The waiter comes. At last, the four friends order lunch. Miranda orders a big bowl of potato soup and a chicken sandwich. Hector orders a large salad, lots of bread, and a glass of water.

Questions

A. Do you understand? Write your answers on a piece of paper.

1. Who arrived at the restaurant first?

2. Who is very, very hungry?

3. Who is a vegetarian? What do vegetarians eat?

B. Word Study. Write your answers.

1. Which words are count nouns?

friend   restaurant   juice   spoon

soup   milk   egg

2. Write what each person orders.

Miranda _____

Rafael _____

Hector _____

C. Check Your Work

Compare your answers with your teacher's answers. Correct your mistakes.